Saving and saving

If you are doing a picture over a period of time, keep all the pieces you are using together—in a bag or envelope, for instance. Then they won't get lost.

It's also a good idea to keep left-over bits and pieces anyway. Many of the projects in this book use scrap materials, so the left-overs are sure to come in useful. If you let people know that you are making a collection, they may be able to add to it with their own odds and ends.

You could keep collections of different kinds of things in separate boxes. Put big labels on the boxes so that you will know what's inside.

---

are good when you want to put paint on firmly.
House-painting brushes are best for large areas.

Glue

PVA glue is a good all-round glue. It can also be thinned with water and used as a varnish. If you splash some on your clothes, wash it out while it's still wet—once it dries, it won't come out. Stik 'n' Fix by Bostik is a PVA glue.
Rubber-based gum, such as Cow Gum, is good for sticking paper. Spread it on one surface only and press. If you get gum where you don't want it, just rub it off.
Clear glue is very strong. It's good for making quick-drying spots of glue. Bostik 1 and UHU are clear glues.

Showing off pictures

Here are two quick and easy ways to display your pictures.
Reusable glue such as Blu-tack by Bostick is like tacky plasticine and holds pictures to walls or to windows. You need only one blob at each corner, and when you want to move the picture, pull it gently off the wall or window taking the glue off at the same time. The glue will leave no mark behind and can be used again.
Sticky tape For sticking pictures to windows, you could use bits of ordinary sticky tape across each corner. But for an invisible join, use double-sided sticky tape.
Never use sticky tape on walls—it will pull off the paint or wallpaper.

TAKE CARE!

An important part of making things is learning to use tools and materials properly.
Scissors should be kept closed when not in use. Work with the tips facing away from your body.
Pins and needles are best kept in a pincushion. Never leave them lying about.
Knives should never be used with the sharp side of the blade facing you. Keep your fingers well away from the blade when you cut things.
Other people's things must be respected. Always ask before you use something that doesn't belong to you.
Now have fun and be safe, too!

Changing country-side

The background in this picture is the only part that is fixed—everything else can be moved around. All the shapes are made of felt. When you put one piece of felt on another, it stays until you peel it off.

▶ You will need:
☐ Pieces of different-coloured felt
☐ Card for background
☐ Pencil, tracing paper
☐ Scissors, pins
☐ PVA glue and spreader

1

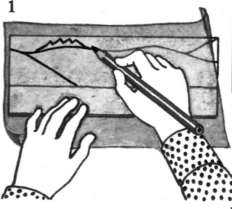

Draw the background on the card. Put in all the things that won't move—fields, sky, mountains, road, and so on.
1. Lay tracing paper on top of the background card, and trace the outlines you've drawn. Write in the colour you want each piece to be on the tracing paper.

2

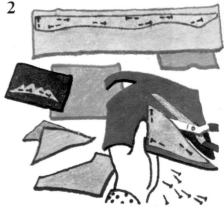

Cut along the lines to separate the different shapes.
2. Pin each paper shape to felt in the right colour, and cut round the paper.
Remove the pins.
Spread glue on the back of the felt pieces and glue in place on the background card.

exciting ways to make
pictures

about this book

This do-it-yourself craft book is specially designed for children. Every page has such clear step-by-step pictures and easy-to-follow words that you can do everything on your own without adult help. And once you see how the projects work, you'll be inspired to make dozens of creative things!

This book shows you lots of ways to make unusual and exciting pictures with everyday materials. The chapters are arranged with the easier projects at the beginning and the more difficult ones at the end. In many cases the methods in one chapter lead on to the methods in the next chapter, so it's a good idea to follow the order of the book.

The blue tag at the side of a page tells you the method used or the things made in that chapter—all the methods or things made between one tag and another are the same or similar.

The 'Try it first' tag at the top of a page indicates a practice section. This gives you a chance to try out a method with a simple project before starting on something bigger.

Before you start, it's helpful to read through the 'Useful things to know' pages overleaf.

Useful things to know

Before you start a project, look through the whole chapter so that you have a picture in your mind of what you are going to do. Then gather the things you will need.

Try to clear as much space to work in as possible. Cover the work-top with newspaper so that it doesn't matter if you make a mess with paints, dyes or glue. Cover yourself up, too, with an apron or overall. Have an old cloth handy so that you can clean your hands as you go along. If you get paint on yourself, wash it off with warm water and washing powder. If you get fabric dye on your clothes, wash them at once. First rinse them in cold water and then wash them with warm water and washing powder.

When you've finished, clear up blobs of paint, dye and glue as quickly as possible. Roll up the newspaper with the messy side inside and throw it away. Always put lids and tops back properly and wash brushes and clean other things you have used.

Optional things

In some of the projects in this book, you will see the word 'optional'. All this means is that you can choose whether or not to use the thing listed.

Paper and card

Instead of buying paper and card, see how many different kinds you can collect at home. Old envelopes and the backs of letters, white exercise paper, paper bags, carrier bags, used wrapping paper, scraps of wallpaper, sweet papers and so on will all come in useful. Keep your eyes open, too, for used postcards, the backs of writing pads, cereal boxes, shoeboxes and cardboard cartons. But only use things that no one wants any more. If you do need to buy paper or card, go to a stationer's or art shop.

Cheap papers are newsprint (unprinted newspaper), shelf or lining paper (used to line wallpaper).

Cartridge paper is better quality, but dearer.

Tissue paper is flimsy and tears easily, so remember to handle it carefully.

Tracing paper can be any kind of see-through paper—greaseproof paper will do.

Card can be bought in various thicknesses. For most projects, though, card found at home will be fine.

Paints

Poster and powder paint are fine for painting paper and card.

Acrylic paint can also be used on paper and card, on top of other kinds of paint and on hard surfaces, such as wood, as well. It dries waterproof, so don't let it dry on your brushes.

All three types of paint can be mixed and cleaned off with water. Use old lids, saucers, or plastic containers for mixing the paint in.

Emulsion paint is the kind used on walls. When it dries, it has a flat, even surface, so it's good for painting large areas. Some emulsion paint is called 'non-drip'—this means that it doesn't drip. Brushes used for emulsion can be cleaned with water and detergent.

Brushes

Choose a brush which is the right type and size for the job.

Small, soft brushes, such as squirrel-hair brushes, are best for painting small, delicate shapes.

Stiff brushes, such as hog's hair brushes or glue brushes,

Now do the movable things. Lay tracing paper over the background and draw simple shapes that will fit in. You could try some that you traced from books or magazines. Cut out the paper shapes.
3. Pin and cut out the felt shapes as before.

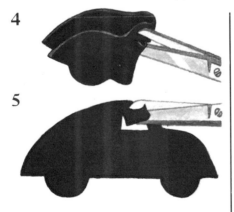

If you have cut a car shape, here's how to make a window. Fold the felt down the middle of the window area.
4. Cut a slit for the bottom of the window, half as wide as you want the window to be.
5. Open out the felt and cut out the rest of the shape.

6. Now arrange the pieces on the background.
When you get tired of the way the picture looks, just peel off the pieces and rearrange them. The truck might transport sheep or felled trees. And, of course, the cars don't all have to go the same way.

Sticker collage

A collage is a picture you build up by sticking things on to a background. The collage on the right is made from self-adhesive stickers. They are called self-adhesive because they already have sticky glue on the back. You can buy stickers like these in stationers' shops. In art shops and toy shops, you will also find packets of paper shapes especially for making pictures. Some are self-adhesive, but others must be moistened with a damp sponge or cloth—or licked with your tongue—before they will stick.

Sticker pattern

► You will need:
☐ Paper for background
☐ Stickers or paper shapes
☐ Damp sponge or cloth for moistening shapes (optional)

1. Press down one sticker in the middle of the paper.

Add a ring of stickers around the first one. Try out different colours and shapes.
2. Now build out the pattern. Fill up the whole of the paper if you want.

Easy pictures

Now try doing a simple picture. Use the same things as for 'Try it first'. If you like, let some stickers overlap to build up bigger shapes, as shown in the picture.

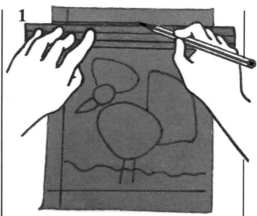

Bigger pictures

For the bird, you will need the same things as before and a ruler to draw a border.
Pencil in the main shapes—the body, head, feathers and so on.
1. Lightly rule a border. It helps to have some straight lines to follow.

2. Now build up your picture, making the most of the different sticker shapes. See how long shapes have been used for head and tail feathers in the bird picture and how a round red shape has been used for the sun.

Shades and shapes

Have you ever been lazily doodling and found that you've drawn lots of times round and round the outline of a shape? By adding different colours or using different shades of colour, you can turn your doodle into a lifelike picture.

This is called 3-D—an effect that makes flat surfaces seem thicker and more shapely. See how the eagle appears to be dipping and soaring across the page. Different colours and shades have been used in a clever way to make it seem real.

Doodle design

Start with a colourful and simple tree. Or make up your own design.

▶ You will need:
☐ Thin coloured card for background, 12cm × 20cm
☐ Thin card to paint on
☐ Poster paint in green and white
☐ Old saucer for mixing paint
☐ A brush, scissors
☐ A pencil, ruler
☐ PVA glue and spreader
☐ Small piece of thick card
☐ Newspaper

Cover your work surface with newspaper.
Cut three shapes from thin card—one 4cm × 6cm, one 6cm × 8cm and one 8cm × 10cm.

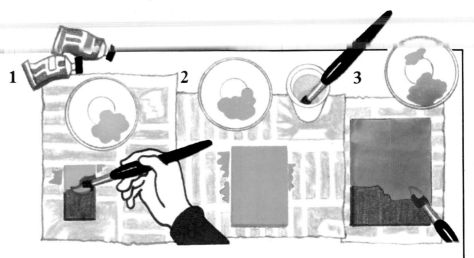

Put white paint in the saucer.
1. Mix in a tiny blob of green paint to get a light green. Paint the smallest card this colour.
If you paint the brush strokes in one direction, the surface will be even when it dries.

2. Add more green paint to the saucer until the colour is a medium-green.
Paint the middle-sized card in this colour.
Wash your brush thoroughly with water. Be sure to rinse out all the paint.
3. Paint the largest card green with no white added.
Let the cards dry completely.

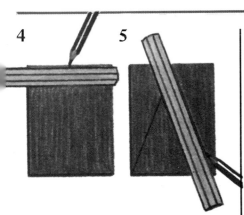

4. Turn the largest card over with the unpainted side up. Measure the top side of the card and put a small mark at the halfway point.
5. Draw lines from the mark to the bottom corners of the card. Do the same for the other cards. Now cut out the three tree shapes.

Turn the darkest green tree painted side up, and glue the medium-green tree on top.
6. Put a dab of glue on the back of the light-green tree. Glue to the medium-green one.
7. Cut a small square of thick card, 2cm × 2cm and glue it in the centre of the background. Spread glue on top of the card square and press the 3-D tree in place.

8. Paint in falling snowflakes, a moon and snowy ground. With the left-over bits, make a tree-trunk. Or give your tree small friends to keep it company until the Christmas season.

The eagle is made the same way as the doodle design. Since it's a big project to paint, use different-coloured paper instead to get the 3-D effect.

Window art with tissue

Have you noticed the stained glass windows in churches? Here's how to get a similar effect with coloured tissue paper. Tearing tissue makes the edges seem more interesting and natural—cut only when tearing is too difficult!

Stick the tissue paper to a transparent material such as polythene. If you can get a box lid with a transparent window, use this—just leave an edge of card round the window to give you a ready-made frame.

Fish in the water

Find out how to do window art with this easy fish picture.

▶ You will need:
- ☐ Different-coloured tissue paper
- ☐ Transparent material for background
- ☐ Rubber-based gum and spreader
- ☐ Drawing paper same size as background
- ☐ Pencil, scissors, paper clips
- ☐ Scrap white paper
- ☐ Reusable glue or sticky tape
- ☐ Dark paper or card for frame (optional)

Draw a rough plan of the picture on the drawing paper. Clip the transparent material over your drawing.

To make the fish's body, fold some tissue paper in half.
1. Tear out half the body shape against the fold, going through both tissue layers. When you open out the paper, the shape will be exactly the same on either side of the fold.

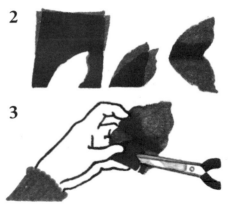

2. To make the eye, fold one end of the body to the middle of the fish. Cut out the eye as shown.
3. Tear out the tail from another piece of tissue. Open the paper out. Don't worry if the shapes are not quite the same as in the drawing—the drawing is only a rough guide.

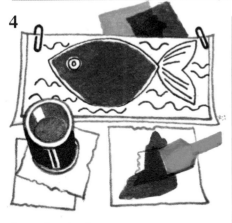

Lay the body on scrap paper and spread gum thinly on it. Be careful not to tear the paper. Turn the body over and stick it to the background, following the drawing underneath. Press it down with clean paper.
4. Stick on the tail.

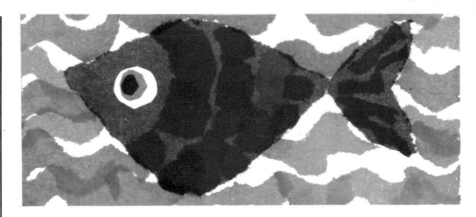

Now that the main shape is in place, remove the paper clips. Tear out and stick on scales. Fill in the spaces with waves. Experiment with overlapping colours. Several layers of one colour will make that colour deeper. Two layers in different colours will make a third colour.

If your picture doesn't already have a frame, you could make one from dark paper or card. Fix your picture to a window with Blu-tack or sticky tape.

Now that you know how to do window pictures, try doing one like the king on the left.

Waste paper parrot

This is a cheap picture to do. It also helps to tidy things up because it's made of waste paper. Start a collection of left-over wrappings, old comics, foil—in fact, any kind of interesting and colourful paper will do.

Think of all the many shapes you can make with your paper. Tear it for things with soft or ragged edges; cut it if you want crisp shapes.

Paper tree

Start with an easy picture of a tree against the sky.

▶ You will need:
- ☐ Scrap paper
- ☐ Card for background
- ☐ Rubber-based gum or PVA glue and spreader
- ☐ Scissors, felt-tipped pen

Glue some paper to the card to make the smooth sky.
1. Tear out woolly clouds and glue these down.
2. Tear out a ragged-looking trunk and some branches, and glue in place.

Cut out the leaves.
3. Draw in the veins with felt-tipped pen and glue to the branches.

Jolly Polly

Do this picture as you did the tree, with the same materials.
1. The first piece to glue to the background is the main branch. This will give you a basic framework to build on.

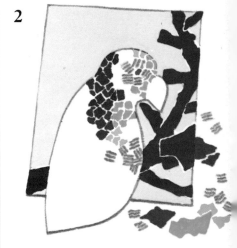

To give the parrot a firm outline, you could first cut its shape in white paper.
2. Then build up the colour on top.
Glue the parrot in place. Add cut-out claws and a tail of pleated paper strips.

sticking cloth

House in a field

Raid the rag bag for bits of cloth, wool, string and braid and make this spring cottage. When doing a cloth collage, choose a subject with a variety of surfaces and textures—some smooth, flat areas and some rough, more patterned ones. Then you can make use of the different look and feel of each of your pieces. In this collage, for instance, flat cloth shows the smoothness of the sky, and knobbly braid and wool coils make the rough soil more real.

Easy flowerpot

Start with a small picture—it need not be more than 12cm × 15cm.

► You will need:
- ☐ Scrap cloth
- ☐ Scraps of wool or string
- ☐ Card for background
- ☐ Cloth for background at least 2cm wider all round than the card
- ☐ PVA glue and spreader
- ☐ Scissors

Lay the background cloth right side down, and place the card in the centre.

Snip the corners of the cloth. Spread glue along the edges of the cloth.
1. Fold the edges over on to the card and press down. Turn the card over and use the front as your background.

Cut out a pot shape from cloth scraps and glue it down. Spread glue on the part where the earth will be. Starting in the middle, wind wool or string round and round to make the earth.
2. Add some flower stalks.
3. Cut flower and leaf shapes and stick these down.

Spring scene

You will need pieces of cloth for the background and all the other things under 'Try it first'.

Divide the background card into the basic areas of sky and ground.
1. Cover each area with a separate piece of cloth.

Cut out cloth shapes for the house, the sun and flowers. Glue on the house and sun. Stick on scraps of wool and string to make the fields.
2. Now add the details. Brighten up the fields by gluing on colourful flowers. Curve and glue brown wool to make the roof tiles.

Tasty fruit you can 'pick'

You could reach out and pluck a grape from this fruit bowl. How are they done to look so real? The secret is a button inside each fruit. Try to find buttons in various sizes—small ones for fruit such as grapes and large ones for fruit like apples.

When choosing cloth to cover the buttons, think about the colour of each fruit and the kind of skin it has. Plums, for instance, have a smooth, slightly shiny skin, so purple velvet would give the right kind of effect.

When you have finished the fruit bowl picture, try to think of ways to use covered buttons in other pictures (see pages 18-19).

You will need:

- ❑ Various buttons
- ❑ Scrap cloth and felt
- ❑ PVA glue and spreader
- ❑ Sewing cotton
- ❑ Scissors
- ❑ Sewing needle
- ❑ Card for background
- ❑ Cloth for background at least 2cm wider all round than the card
- ❑ Different-coloured embroidery thread or wool (optional)

Covering a button

1. Lay a piece of cloth right side down and put a button on top. The cloth should be at least three times as wide as the button.

2. Pull the cloth to the back of the button and twist tightly.

3. Wind cotton round and round the twist, and knot it firmly.

4. Cut away the excess cloth without cutting into the twist. Turn your button into anything you like—perhaps a flower or a face.

5. Glue on cloth petals for a flower.

6. Add cloth hair for a face, and sew little stitches for eyes, nose and mouth.

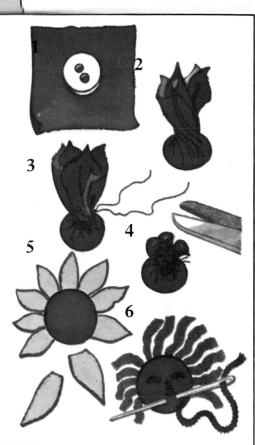

Starting the picture

Cover as many buttons as you want for your fruit.

1. Then cut out the other parts of the picture from felt or cloth.

Make the bowl any shape you like. Cut curved bananas and little leaves and stalks.

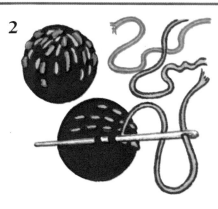

2. You could add colourful details with stitches in embroidery thread. Tiny yellow stitches, for instance, will look like strawberry pips. You could also add details, like the shine on a cherry, by sticking on bits of cloth.

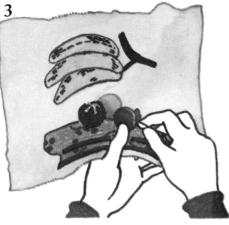

Glue the bowl to the background cloth.

3. Add the other pieces. Heavy fruit may have to be fixed with a few stitches, too.

Stretch the background cloth over the card (see page 14) and your collage is all buttoned up.

Magic box

What's behind this door? Open it—and you will see children playing football in the park. This picture is made up of all kinds of bits and pieces. You will already know how to use most of them if you have done the earlier projects in the book. The only really new things are the tiny people. Practise making these first before going on to do the whole picture.

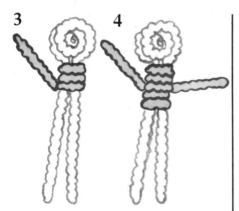

3. Wrap another pipe-cleaner round for the neck. Let the end stick out to make an arm.
4. Do the other arm and body. Trim arms to the same length, and legs too, if necessary.

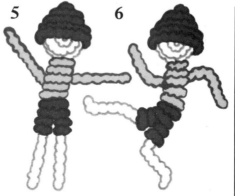

5. Wind on some trousers and add a scarf or hat.
6. Bend the person into action.

Into the box

▶ You will need:
- ☐ Box with hinged lid
- ☐ Scrap cloth and paper
- ☐ Curtain tape
- ☐ Pipe-cleaners
- ☐ Button, cotton wool
- ☐ PVA glue and spreader or table knife
- ☐ Scissors, felt-tipped pen
- ☐ Button for door-knob

Decide where you want the grass and the sky, and cut these parts from cloth or paper. Make the pieces wide enough to cover the sides of the box too.
Glue the pieces in place, cutting out a square at each corner to make a neat fold.

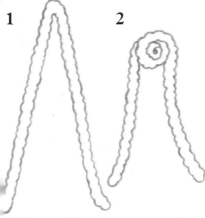

Pipe-cleaner people

You will need pipe-cleaners (in
different colours if possible)
and some scissors.

1. Fold a pipe-cleaner in half.
2. Loop it round several times
at the fold to make the head.

Now add cotton wool clouds.
Put blobs of glue on the sky
and press the clouds on top.
Glue on buildings cut from
paper or cloth. Checked cloth
would be good for windows.
1. Add a tape fence.

Make some pipe-cleaner
people—you could use the one
you made for 'Try it first'.
For the ball, cover a button
with cloth (see page 17). Glue
on the people and the ball.
Cut out cloth or paper flowers.
2. Spread glue on the flowers
and stick them in place.

Last of all, do the door.
Cover the lid with coloured
paper and draw in the details
with felt-tipped pen.
3. Glue on a button for the
door-knob.

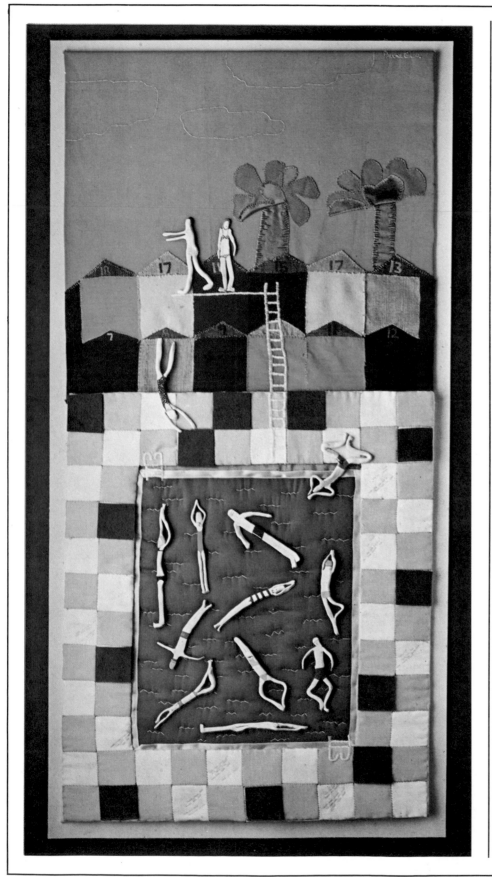

Making a splash!

Here's a way of making a picture come alive. Add little clay people, diving and swimming on a hot summer's day, to a flat picture background and hey presto—can you hear them splishing and splashing in the pool? The background can be as simple or as complicated as you like. You could cut a colour photo or a scene from a magazine. Or make a background like the one in the photograph which combines gluing, sewing, patchwork and embroidery.

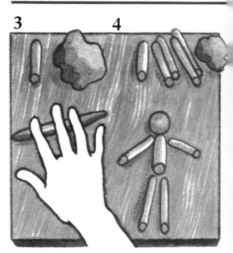

Now comes the exciting bit!
3. Make a little sausage of clay for the body of each swimmer.
4. Add a ball for the head and thinner sausages for the arms and legs.
Look at the photograph for ideas for shapes of swimming, diving and standing people.

Two swimmers

In this picture, the background is made by gluing on scraps of paper and cloth and then adding the 3-D people.

▶ You will need:
- ☐ Scraps of cloth and paper in different colours
- ☐ Piece of card the size you want the picture to be
- ☐ Poster paint, bright blue for sky and various colours for swimmers
- ☐ Pencil, felt-tipped pen
- ☐ Scissors, pins
- ☐ PVA glue and spreader for background
- ☐ Clear glue for clay people
- ☐ Self-hardening clay (such as DAS)
- ☐ A brush

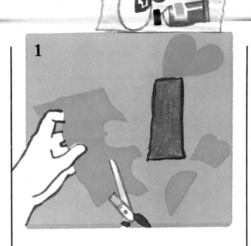

Paint the piece of card all over with the blue poster paint. This will show through as the sky and the water.

1. Using the scraps of paper and cloth, cut out the tree-trunk and some leaf shapes (in different greens, if possible). Stick them on to the background in the right place.

Cut out three different-coloured rectangles for the huts and three triangular roofs in contrasting colours. Stick them down 'in front' of the tree. Use the felt-tipped pen to mark in the number of each hut.

2. Now glue on the paved path, using a piece of checked cloth or squares of different-coloured paper.

5. Let the people dry hard, and then paint on their costumes. Leave the paint to dry.

6. To finish the picture, glue the people in place. Make sure the glue is really dry before moving the picture.

The large pool

If you're ambitious, how about trying out some of the ideas shown in the photograph? The huts and the paving stones are stitched together as patchwork and then sewn to the blue cloth sky. The trees have been appliquéd to the sky with big embroidery stitches. You can use more embroidery stitches for the clouds, numbers and the diving board.

Cowboy on the cover

Draw a swing door shape on the front of a small cereal packet. Cut out the space at the top and bottom of the doors, then cut the centre of the doors to open them. Make a clay cowboy and glue him in in the box.

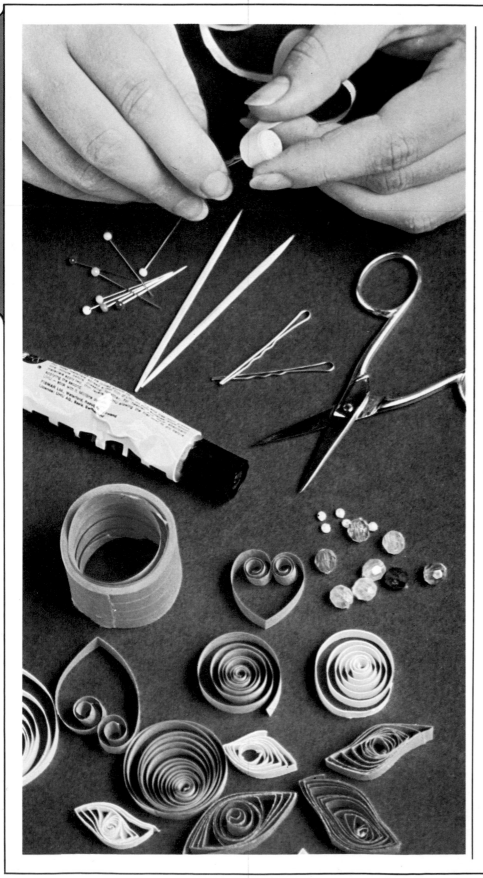

The art of quilling

Quilling is a very old way of making pictures and decorations with rolled paper strips. At one time, the paper was rolled round a quill—this is the name for a slit feather used as a pen. Quilling is an ideal pastime for a rainy day when you feel like doing something quiet.

Tear-drops and eyes

For a tear-drop shape, first make a loose round coil. Then pinch the glued end to form a point.
For an eye shape, pinch a round coil to form two points opposite each other.

Making basic shapes

► You will need:
- ☐ Different-coloured paper strips about 1cm × 20 cm
- ☐ Hair-grip with the ends cut off (see photograph)
- ☐ PVA glue
- ☐ Toothpick, cocktail stick or used matchstick for spreading glue

If you can get some party streamers, you won't have to cut the paper strips by hand. And don't try to cut the ends off the hair-grip yourself—ask an adult to do this for you with a pair of pliers.

1

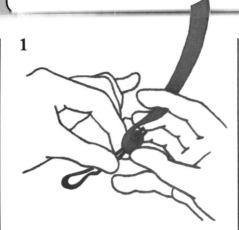

Simple round coil

Slide the end of a paper strip into the hair-grip.
1. Turning the hair-grip, roll the paper round and round.

2

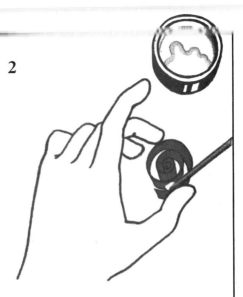

Slide the little roll off the hair-grip.
For a small coil, leave the paper tightly rolled.
For a bigger, looser coil, let the strip unwind a little.
2. Fix the loose end of the coil with a blob of glue.

Leaves

Make this like an eye shape, but squeeze the round coil so that the centre is flattened as well.
Curl the points in opposite directions with your fingers.

Scrolls and hearts

For a scroll, use an unglued round coil.
Unwind half of it, and then roll this end up.
A heart is a scroll squeezed to a point in the middle.

Two letter shapes

For a V-shape, turn a scroll inside out and pinch the middle to a point.
For an S-shape, roll half a strip in one direction, and then roll the other half in the opposite direction.

Quilled pictures

Once you have tried out the basic shapes on pages 22-23, you can make unusual pictures by gluing these shapes on to card. You could experiment and vary the shapes to suit your picture. Try out different lengths of paper to make the pieces bigger, smaller, looser or tighter.

Keep your picture fairly simple—it will look more dramatic if it isn't cluttered! When you glue on the pieces, put glue only on part of each one. This makes the picture less messy. It also leaves the rest of each piece free, and the coils hold their natural shape better.

Snails on a journey

This family of snails on a Sunday outing is an easy picture to start with.

▶ You will need:
☐ 1cm wide paper strips
☐ Hair-grip with ends cut off
☐ Card for background (ready-coloured, otherwise painted)
☐ Scissors
☐ PVA glue
☐ Toothpick, cocktail stick or used matchstick for spreading glue

Cut three strips for the shells and three for the heads and bodies. The shell strips should vary in length a little, the biggest twice as long as the head and body strips.

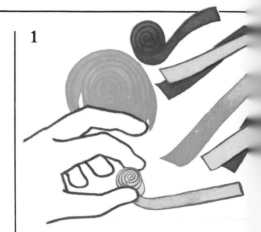

1

Make loose coils for the shells and glue down the ends.
1. Roll a strip into a tight coil for the head, leaving a long, straight end for the body.

2

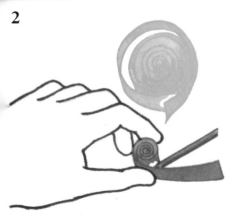

3

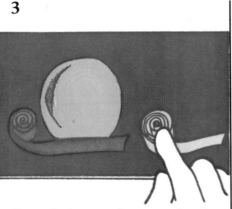

2. Put a blob of glue on the back of each head and body just where the coils end. This will stop the coils unrolling. Spread glue on the back of the head and press the body on to the card.

Spread glue on the central coils at the back of each shell.
3. Press the shells in place above the tail.
Put a dot of glue on the bottom of the shell and press the tail to it.
Make the other snails in the same way.

More ideas

Create other quilled pictures like the ones below. They all use some basic shapes but include variations too.
The tortoise has a shell made from round coils pinched into three or four points.
The dragonfly uses an inside-out scroll for antennae.
The fish has a tear-drop tail. The curve has been folded in half to make two points.
The face uses a leaf variation for the mouth.
When doing pictures of more complicated things like these, work from the middle outwards. What other shapes of your own can you invent?

Shadow portraits

Here is a crafty and quick way to make amazing likenesses of your friends. Simply draw round the shadow of a person's face on to dark paper, and then cut out your drawing. The proper name for this kind of solid shape or outline is 'silhouette'.

Doing portraits like these was once very popular—you may even see some old ones in museums or antique shops.

▶ You will need:
- ☐ A friend who will sit still
- ☐ A chair for your friend
- ☐ A table lamp without a shade
- ☐ Paper, light on one side and dark on the other (painted, if necessary)
- ☐ Light-coloured paper or card for backgrounds to silhouettes
- ☐ Reusable glue
- ☐ Pencil, scissors
- ☐ Rubber-based gum and spreader

Seat your friend facing sideways as close to the wall as possible.

1. Arrange the lamp so that a sharp shadow of your friend is cast on the wall.

Turn off any other lights to make the shadow as clear as possible.

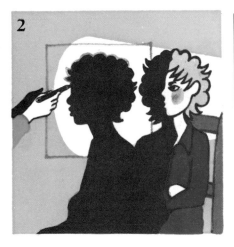

Blu-tack a sheet of paper to the wall, white side uppermost, so that the whole shadow falls inside.

2. Carefully draw round the edge of the shadow.

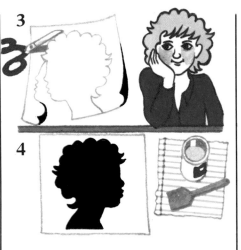

When you have finished, take the drawing down, and let your friend breathe again.

3. Cut out the silhouette and turn over the paper.

4. Stick the silhouette on to the background paper or card.

Group portraits

Try doing some portraits of your family or a group of your friends. You could use different-coloured paper for each person and arrange the portraits so that they overlap.

Shapes against the light

You can make silhouettes of anything, not just portraits. Draw or trace animals, trees, buildings or people and cut them out as flat, dark shapes. They will look very effective hanging in the window light. For a really grand finish, do a round picture—the lampshade on page 31. It looks quite ordinary with the light off—but when you turn the light on, a hidden city springs to life!

Shadow show

Entertain your friends with a moving picture show. Try making up a story about two cats (like the one in the witch picture) who meet high on the rooftops. They will appear to move around and 'miaow' on their own.

First, fix up your theatre and rehearse your performance. It's best to work in a darkened room.

▶ You will need:
- ☐ A large cardboard box
- ☐ A lamp which can be directed or one without a shade
- ☐ A mirror (optional)
- ☐ A sheet of thin white paper
- ☐ Card (cornflakes box will do)
- ☐ Pencil, scissors
- ☐ Knitting needles or sticks
- ☐ Transparent sticky tape

Cut up the cardboard box so that you just have three sides. Cut a 'window' about 32cm × 35cm in the centre panel.
1. Tape a piece of white paper over the back of the window to make the screen. Cut the paper larger than the window.

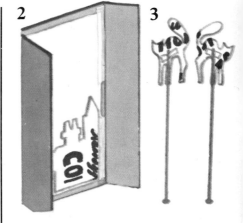

On card draw and cut out the rooftop scenery.
2. Tape it in position to the back of the white paper screen. Draw and cut out two card cats, each about 10cm tall.
3. Tape a knitting needle 'control rod' to each cat's back.

Witching time

Try starting with a picture that's not too complicated like this twilight witch.

▶ You will need:
- ☐ Pale blue tissue paper, thin white paper, black paper and drawing paper all the same size
- ☐ Pencil, small pointed scissors
- ☐ Rubber-based gum and spreader
- ☐ Sticky tape

First, plan your picture.
Draw the witch and things you want to show on the drawing paper.
Tape your drawing over the black paper.
1. Cut round the outlines through both layers of paper. Hold the layers together as you cut.

Tape the blue tissue paper to the thin white paper.
2. Glue the black shapes on to the pale blue background.
Frame your picture with black paper and fix it to the window with 'Blu-tack or sticky tape.

Put the stage on a table.
4. Switch on a light behind it and direct the light on to the white paper screen.
Position the light so that when you give your show the light will still shine on the screen.
If you have a mirror, arrange it where the audience will be.
Then you can see what effects you are creating for the audience.

5. Tell the story of these rooftop cats while making them jump about, or have a 'miaowing duet' behind the screen.
If you hold a cat very near the screen, its shadow will be clear, small and dark.
If you move it back towards the light, the shadow will be big, pale and furry.

The town at night

This picture is a little more complicated than the last one because you have to cut out windows and wing lights. The picture can be drawn freehand or traced from this book.

▶ You will need:
☐ Thin white paper, and drawing or tracing paper, all the same size
☐ Black paper
☐ Tissue paper in pale blue, yellow, red and green
☐ Pencil, small pointed scissors
☐ Rubber-based gum and spreader
☐ Sticky tape, ruler
☐ Black felt-tipped pen

5

5. Stick yellow tissue behind the windows and green and red behind the wings.
Glue the pieces to the blue background.
When the glue is dry, draw in the dividing lines between the windows with felt-tipped pen.
You could also add spires on top of buildings.

1

Draw or trace your picture.
To trace it, lay tracing paper over the page.
1. Trace as many of each shape as you want, and extend the buildings if you like by drawing straight lines.
Go over your drawing or tracing with felt-tipped pen to make the outlines really clear.

2

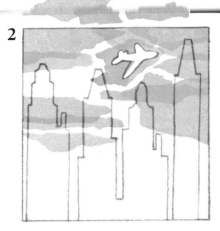

Lay thin white paper over your drawing or tracing. Slip more white paper under the tracing if the lines are hard to see.
2. Build up the sky with blue tissue strips (see page 11). Leave a space for the plane so that when you stick the pieces down, the yellow windows will be against white paper.

3

4

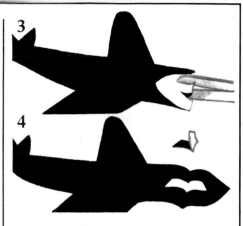

Use your drawing or tracing to cut out the black shapes.
For windows, fold the paper down the middle of a window area.
3. Cut a rectangle against the fold as long as the window or row of windows but only half as wide.
4. Then open the paper out. Do the wing lights like the fish's eye on page 11.

Lampshade magic

If you had fun making the skyscraper picture, why not use the idea to line a lampshade. When the light is off—there's only a plain shade. Switch it on—and the skyscraper city comes to life.

▶ You will need:
- ☐ Straight-sided shade in a pale colour
- ☐ All the materials in 'The town at night'
- ☐ Sheet of white paper long enough to go round shade
- ☐ Measuring tape, ruler
- ☐ Clothes pegs

1

2

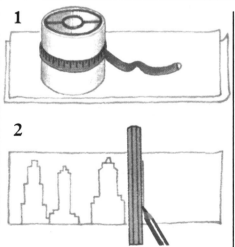

1. Measure round the shade and add 2cm to the length. Measure the height, too. Draw a rectangle this size on white paper. Cut it out.
2. Make a skyscraper picture across the white paper. Leave a plain strip 2cm wide at one end.

3

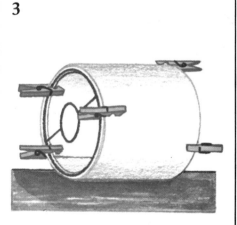

Spread gum round the inside edges of the shade.
Roll your design up with the picture facing outwards. Unroll it inside the shade and press it against the gum. Stick the overlapping join down.
3. Peg it all until the gum has dried. Remove the pegs.

Sparkling pictures

Here's a fascinating way to make pictures by painting on glass. Put paint on the back of the glass, and then glue crumpled kitchen foil behind it. Since most glass paint colours are transparent, the foil shines through and makes them glow. Where there is no paint at all, the foil looks sparkling silver. You paint these pictures back to front—the paint you put on first will be on top of the other colours when you turn the glass over.

2 3

4

5

2. Turn the dish upside down on the paper, and draw round it.

3. Remove the dish and draw a bold, simple pattern on the paper. Remember that you will be copying this on to the back of the glass, so the pattern will be the other way round when you turn the glass over.

Lay the dish upside down over the drawing. Move the dish if necessary so that the drawing lies under the part you want to paint.

4. Copy the outline of the drawing on to the back of the dish using black paint. (When you have finished painting the dish and you turn it over, the black outline will be on top of the other colour.)

5. When the outline is dry, fill in the transparent colour, but leave some bits unpainted so that the foil backing can show through.

Painted dish

Practise by painting a shallow glass dish, saucer or an ashtray. If the ashtray has some advertising words on it, you can try removing them with a bit of cotton wool and white spirit or nail polish remover. Do this on newspaper—never on wood or Formica.

You need special transparent glass paint which you can buy at craft shops. As well as a transparent colour, you will need black and white paint which is opaque—this means that you can't see through it. If you can't get opaque paint, use enamel paint instead—the kind used for painting models.

► You will need:
- ☐ Clear glass dish, saucer or ashtray
- ☐ Transparent glass paint in red, blue or yellow
- ☐ Black opaque glass or enamel paint
- ☐ Medium-sized soft paintbrush
- ☐ Paper, pencil, clear glue
- ☐ Kitchen foil, scissors
- ☐ Washing-up liquid
- ☐ Rag without any fluff
- ☐ Glass paint thinner
- ☐ White spirit for enamel paint, if needed

You will need glass paint thinner for cleaning your brushes. White spirit will clean off enamel paint.

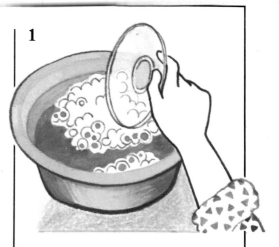

1

1. Wash the dish well with hot water and washing-up liquid. Rinse it, and dry it with the rag.
From now on, try to hold the dish by the edge only so that you won't get finger-marks all over it.

6

When all the paint is completely dry, cover the back of the dish with foil. The shiny side of the foil should be against the paint.
6. Glue the foil to the edge of the dish.
Trim off any bits of foil that stick out beyond the dish.

Now turn the dish over. See how the black lines seem to stand out in front of the other colour.
Try painting other designs and patterns on glass. Brighten up jars and glasses—use them as pencil holders or vases for dried flowers.

Frosty scene

► You will need:
☐ All the things under 'Try it first', except the dish
☐ Transparent glass paint in red, blue and yellow
☐ A table knife
☐ Glass to paint on*
☐ Coloured sticky tape (optional)

*A small ready-made picture frame with glass inside would be ideal. Just take the glass out for painting, and put it back when you have finished. Department stores and do-it-yourself shops sell frames like this.
Remember: glass can cut you! Carry it carefully and don't run your fingers along the edges.

1

Clean the glass as before. Do a drawing like the one in the photographs. Remember that everything in the final painting will be the other way round.
1. Paint in black outlines wherever you want them, such as on the doors and the windows.

2

2. When the black paint is dry, paint in any parts that you want completely white. Follow your drawing which you can see through the glass.

For coloured highlights, as on the trees, wipe away part of the top colour while it is still wet.
4. Paint in the house. You can use red and blue to make purple as on the roof. When all the colours are dry, turn your picture over and lay it on a sheet of foil. Does it need more silver 'moonlight' in the clouds or on the hills? If so, turn it back again and carefully use the knife to scrape away parts of the paint so that the foil can show through.

4

3. When the white paint is dry, start to fill in the other colours as shown in the photograph. Build them up in layers until you get the strength of the colour you want. Leave each layer to dry before painting the next one.

Remember not to paint over the parts of the picture you want the silver foil to show through—the moon, the windows, the road and so on. If you put one colour on top of another, you can get a third colour. Blue on yellow, for example, will give you green as in the trees. White on a thin layer of blue will make pale blue as in the door.

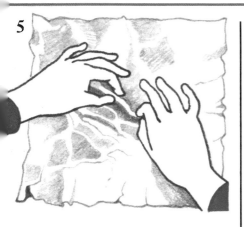

Cut a piece of foil at least 3cm bigger all round than the glass.
5. Squeeze and crumple it to suit different parts of the picture. Long, thin creases look good behind grass. Bigger, more uneven creases work well behind the sky.

Put blobs of glue along the edge of the foil, and press it on to the glass. When the glue is dry, trim the edges of the foil.
6. Put the glass painting back in the frame and fix the backing.

7. If you don't have a frame, bind the edges with coloured sticky tape.

painting cloth

People in design

Make a really colourful and personal bedcover by painting your silhouette on a sheet. When you put the cover on your bed, it will be quite clear who sleeps there! While you work, it would be a good idea to close the door so that the cat or your baby sister can't come in and walk all over the wet dye! To avoid unwanted marks on the cloth, stand the dye on a piece of newspaper while you work. And, of course, remember to ask for the tea-towel or old sheet before you start painting because the dye won't wash out.

Handy tea-towel

Here's an idea for practising with fabric dyes and drawing round things at the same time.

► You will need:
☐ A plain tea-towel
☐ Fabric dye (such as Dylon 'Color-fun' fabric paint)
☐ A big brush
☐ A pencil
☐ Newspapers
☐ An iron

Lay the tea-towel on newspaper. This will stop the dye from staining the floor or table top.
1. Put your hand on the tea-towel and draw round it with the pencil. Move it about and draw round it several more times until you have made an interesting pattern.

2. Paint in the hands with fabric dye.
Or, if you like, you can paint in designs or paint them different colours.

3. When the dye feels dry, hang the tea-towel up somewhere to dry out completely.
If you splash fabric dye on your clothes, wash it out immediately with cold water.
Be sure to wash your brushes in water before the dye dries.

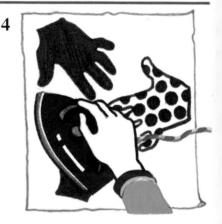

4. To fix the dye so that the painted tea-towel can be washed, it must be ironed several times with a hot iron. Ask an adult to do this for you, or ask if you may do it yourself.

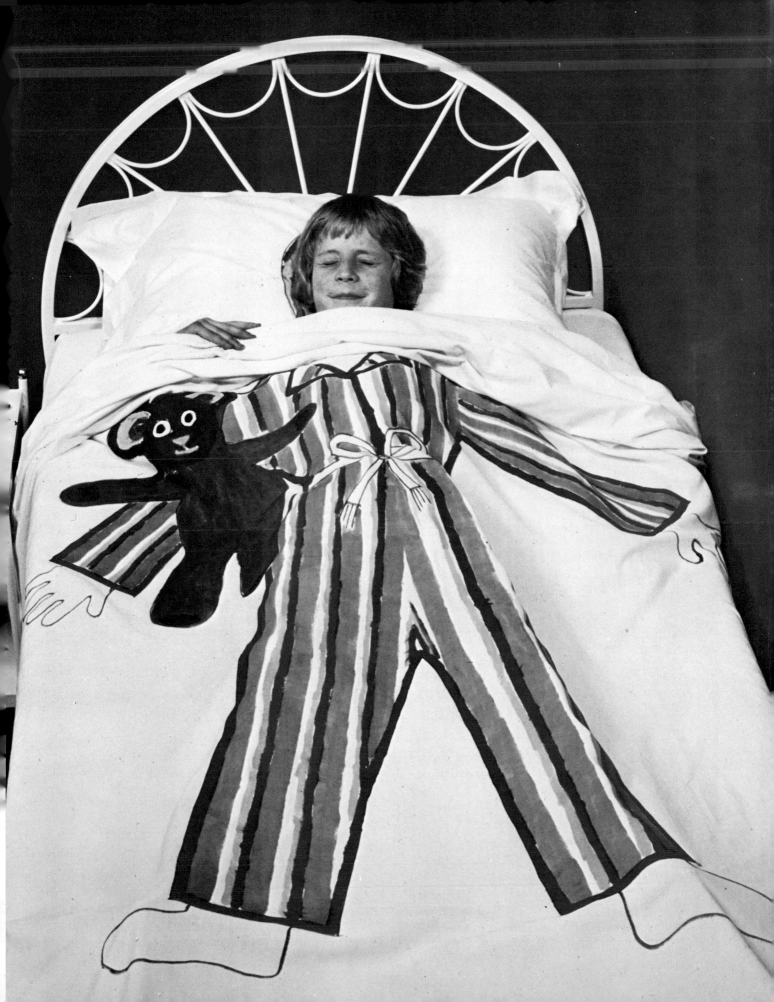

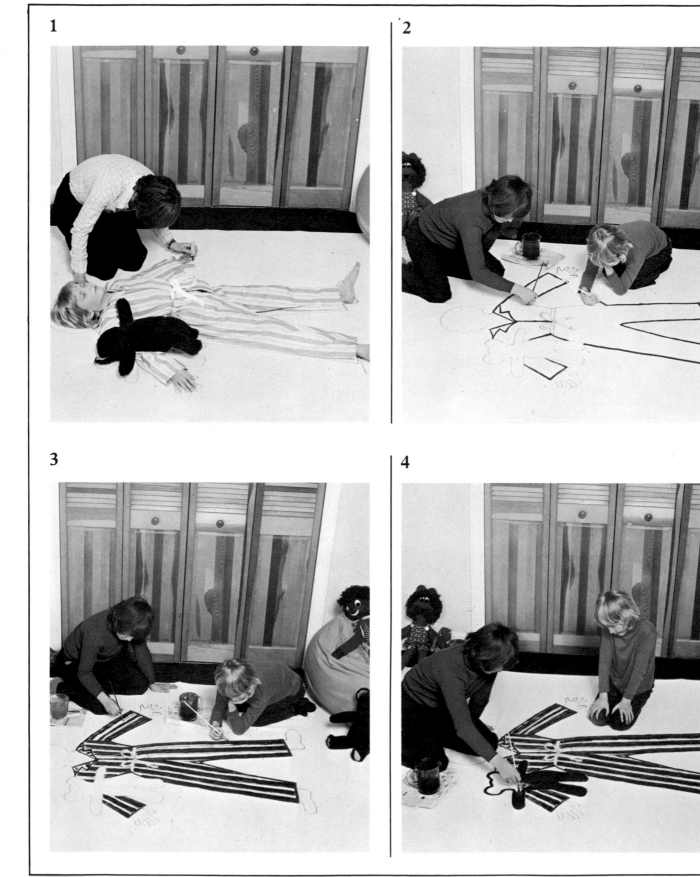

Sleeping beauty

You do this in just the same way as the tea-towel. The photographs on the left show the main steps to follow.
You will need all the things under 'Try it first' (except the tea-towel) plus fabric dyes in two or three colours and an old sheet. You will also need a friend to help you.
Make sure you have plenty of floor space before you begin.
First of all, the sheet must be ironed to make it smooth enough to paint on.
Next, lay newspaper all over the floor space where you will be working.

Now change into your night clothes.
Spread the sheet out and lie down in the middle, with a favourite toy if you like.
1. Keep very still while your friend draws round you.
Then get up and change back into your working clothes.
2. Paint over the outline. Hold the sheet as still as possible or the dye might smudge.
3. Fill in the main areas.
4. Then add the details. Paint your face with the eyes closed so that people can see that you're asleep. Remember that the sheet must be ironed when the dye has dried.

When you pull the bedcover up, you'll see a life-sized picture of a sleeping you.

Door portrait

If you can't get hold of a sheet, how about making your mark on your bedroom door?
But remember to ask an adult before you begin.
If you use poster paints on a gloss painted door, the paint should wash off.

Mirror reflection

Draw on a mirror with a wax pencil, an old lipstick or a wax eyebrow pencil.
Stand in front of the mirror and paint what you see. Now take your reflection away.
It might not look exactly like you, but it's a good way to see the proportions of your face.
Clean the mirror with window or mirror cleaner.

Pillow print

Make a matching pillow case to go with your silhouette sheet.
Draw the shape of your head in the middle of the case with a pencil.
Paint over the outline with fabric dye and fill in the details.
After the case has dried, ask an adult to iron it for you.

Mural of circles

Everything in this mural, or wall painting, is made up of circles and curves. Not one of the shapes had been drawn freehand. The rabbit, the flowers, the tree-tops and the clouds have all been done by drawing round different-sized circular objects. The bigger shapes, such as the rainbow, have been drawn with a special string method. The tree-trunks are the only straight shapes in the picture and these have been drawn with a ruler.

Why not try giving your room this professional-looking but simple decoration?

Start with some circle pictures on paper. Choose different objects to draw round for different-sized circles. Bottle-tops and coins, for instance, will make tiny circles, like the rabbit's nose in the photograph. Yogurt pots and plates will make medium-sized circles, and round trays and polythene bowls will make even bigger ones.

▶ You will need:
☐ Paper
☐ Objects to draw round
☐ String, drawing pin, rubber
☐ Ruler, pencil, paintbrush
☐ Poster or powder paint

First decide what to put in each picture and lightly draw in all the parts. Then fill in the shapes with paint.

Single circles

Here's how to do an easy apple tree.
Draw round something large to make the leafy tree-top.
Draw the trunk with a ruler.
Add lots of round apples.

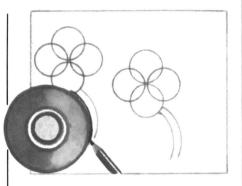

Curvy shapes

For a flower, first mark where you want the centre to be.
Then draw four circles the same size, all touching the centre.
Add a stalk by drawing round part of something to give you two parallel curves.

Draw the edges of clouds and curvy tree-tops with rows of curves.
Use one object to draw round, and move it along as you go.
Don't try to make all the curves the same size—they will be much more interesting if they are different!

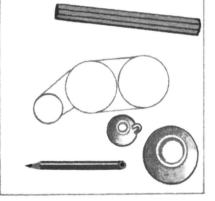

Oblongs

Make oblongs, such as the body of a sheep, by drawing two circles the same size next to each other.
Add a circle for the head.
Then join up the circles with straight lines.

Do the sheep's wool in the same way as the clouds, but use something smaller to draw round. Draw in the legs with a ruler.

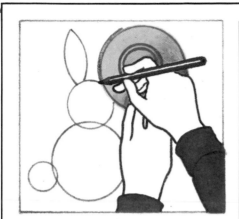

Pointed ovals

For a furry rabbit, start by doing different-sized circles for head, body and tail.
Then do his ears.
For each one, draw two curves which meet at the top. Do leaves in the same way.

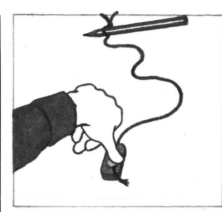

Big circles

For really big circles and curves, as in hills and rainbows, use string, a pencil, a drawing pin and a rubber.
Tie the string to the pencil.
1. Pin the other end to the rubber at the point which will be the centre of the circle.

Hold the drawing pin and rubber down.
2. Pull the string tight and swing the pencil round to draw a curve.
The rubber stops the pin making a hole in the paper.

3. Now draw all the shapes properly. For very big curves, ask a friend to hold the drawing pin while you draw. When you have finished drawing, rub out all unnecessary lines.

Now start painting. Work from the top to the bottom so that you can cover up any drips.
4. Outline an area with paint, using a brush about 2cm wide. Pull the brush along on its side rather than on its tip.

5. Fill in the shape with a bigger brush.
Paint the rest of the picture in the same way.
When you have finished with one colour, clean the brushes properly or you will mess up the next colour. Pale colours may need two or three coats.

Painting the wall

Ask first if you can paint your mural. Then try to get some friends to join in—the more people there are, the less each one will have to do!

If possible, use non-drip paint because it doesn't drip. And don't worry if you cannot get the colours in the photograph—just use any you like.

▶ You will need:
- ☐ Emulsion paint in white and any other colours you want
- ☐ House-painting brushes in various sizes
- ☐ Newspaper
- ☐ Rags for cleaning up
- ☐ All the things under 'Try it first' except paint

1. First paint the wall with white emulsion. If the colour underneath still shows through, add one or two more coats of paint. Let each coat dry thoroughly before adding the next one.

2. Roughly pencil in the main parts of your design on the wall. Then, when you do the final drawing, you will know where everything goes and how big to make each shape. For a really big thing, like a hill, just mark where you want the top to be.

Autumn scene

If you don't like the springtime colours used in the photograph, why not try colours like these to make an autumn scene?

Other ideas

There are lots of other ways to use your emulsion paints for circle pictures. Brighten up an old cupboard with this sheep in the snow or decorate your school case with a good 'all-round owl'!

Pictures from pictures